Failure

Russ Parker

Deputy Director, Acorn Christian Healing Trust

GROVE BOOKS LIMITED

BRAMCOTE NOTTINGHAM NG9 3DS

Contents

I would like to dedicate this booklet to the memory of Bert Boyd. Though he suffered the loss of many things, he did not sow the good seed sparingly. He died on 3rd October 1987 and his going was painful but faithful. However, he was a good teacher and friend to many young people from Birkenhead including us, people who were looking for a meaning to life. He did not fail his friends: thanks, Bert.

I would like to thank all who have helped me write this booklet, in particular my wife Carole who has always been my best listener and Yvonne Fantom who has patiently typed my scribblings into something much more presentable.

No Scar?

Hast thou no scar?
No hidden scar on foot, or side, or hand?
I hear thee sung as mighty in the land,
I hear them hail thy bright ascendant star,
Hast thou no scar?
Hast thou no wound?
Yet I was wounded by the archers, spent,
Leaned me against a tree to die; and rent
By ravening beasts that compassed me, I swooned:
Hast thou no wound?
No wound? no scar?
Yet, as the master shall the servant be,
And pierced are the feet that follow me;
But thine are whole: can he have followed far
Who has nor wound nor scar?

Amy Wilson Carmichael

The Cover Illustration is by Lorna Brabin-Smith

Copyright Russ Parker 1987
First Impression 1987
Reprinted May 1995
ISSN 0262-799X
ISBN 1 85174 066 X

1
Introduction

I can remember how I felt when I stood in the queue at my local post office in Birkenhead waiting to cash in my unemployment giro. Because the amount I was receiving was in excess of £40, I had to produce proof of identity and so I was going to show my driver's licence. The problem was that my licence mentioned the fact that I was a 'Reverend.' My mind raced over such questions as 'Will the lady at the counter notice?' 'What will she think of a Minister being unemployed?' The moment came and I handed over my giro and licence. Did I imagine it, or was she giving me a withering look of cynical disbelief and amusement? I wilted under the stare and felt obliged to blurt out the fact that I was a lay pastor but had been made redundant from my secular job. She gave me one of those sweet smiles which in effect said 'Pull the other one.' By the time I got outside I was feeling quite guilty and just wanted to scream out my anger to God for allowing me to be in this predicament. Like many Christians, I was sure that God would not let me suffer failure in public!

No amount of argument would have convinced me then that I had not failed. What made it more difficult was that I belonged to an evangelical and charismatic spirituality which left little room for failure. Once baptized with the Holy Spirit and power there followed the expectation that the fruits of Pentecost would be infallibly repeated in my life and ministry. The reality turned out to be a sharp contrast; I remained unemployed for over two years during which time my wife gave birth to our son but suffered a severe post-natal depression afterwards. Consequently, far from reaping a harvest of power, I struggled to look after two small children and help my wife recover from her illness. We managed to keep up the mortgage payments on the house, but saw the church actually go into decline and eventually close. In the meantime I got deeper into depression as I wrestled with God to do something and bail me out of my predicament. Yet, to be honest, what I found most difficult to live with was what my friends would think of my lack of success. All the so-called promise of early youth had evaporated. I had been involved with a number of Christian ministries that had been effective, such as the *Come Together*[1] celebrations, but now I felt as if I had been dumped in some lost cause. My pride was hurting, but, like so many people today, I expected success and treated the absence of it as failure.

---

[1] *Come Together* is the title of a musical celebration of worship and fellowship that had its original UK tour in 1973. It gave birth to local groups producing a number of performances all over the country and was one of the resources for church renewal and evangelism in the mid-1970s. It also fostered interest in a number of celebration ministries, the most well-known being Spring Harvest.

2

Everyone Loves a Winner

We live in a society that glamorizes success but has not learnt to deal with its failures. When someone wins a fabulous amount of money on the National Lottery or the football pools they are eagerly photographed receiving the outsize cheque from a TV celebrity. It is as if the rest of the hopefuls in the community can in some way share vicariously in the victory of the winner. However, the anger which explodes in various inner city areas, affecting black or West Indian communities, is dismissed as vandalism and calculated racist demonstrations. The appalling poverty and high percentage of unemployment is somehow glossed over.

There was talk, after the 1987 General Election, of a purge of the leftist influences within the Labour party because it had been defeated three times in a row by the Conservatives under the leadership of Margaret Thatcher. The Alliance rushed into moves to bring about a merger of its two parties, the Liberals and the Social Democrats. They had failed, like Labour, to secure a big enough share of the electorate. All the talk of the success of a third party was suddenly lost in a wave of recriminations concerning the charisma or otherwise of the two leaders. There is no forgiveness for failure, because, it seems, it should not happen.

When the 1987-88 football season opened, it was marked with fierce fighting among fans at the Scarborough versus Wolves match. It was reported that the fighting was caused by disgruntled Wolves fans who felt frustrated that their team had sunk to the fourth division. They did not know how to cope with their feelings of failure.

Consider how much of our entertainment takes the form of competitions and quizzes. Millions of people watch such programmes and enjoy the challenge of matching up their knowledge with the current champions. Competing has become a way of life. We were recently shown on the 'Late Clive James Show' the ridiculous lengths competitors in some Japanese game shows will go to in order to win the prize. On one occasion they were dragged along the rough ground on their backsides and the winner was the one to survive the longest. Winning was all that mattered. Yet the sad fact of life is that there are a lot more casualties than we care to admit. Thousands have died in Britain alone as a result of AIDS. Suicide is now ranked as the eighth major cause of death in the Western hemisphere.[2] One of the major reasons given for this is that people have lost a reason for living and cannot cope with the collapse of their hopes. Our own national statistics inform us that approximately fifty per cent of all mar-

---

2   Articles entitled 'Suicide in America' in *Reader's Digest*, 1984.

riages now end in divorce within the first ten years. Counselling figures reveal that there is an alarming rise in the number of people suffering with depression. Our society, it seems, knows how to encourage success but has not taught its members how to cope with failed expectations. This same imbalance of approach is also found within the Christian world.

There is the general intolerance in some Pentecostal circles to accept continuing sickness after prayer ministry. The sufferers are often made to feel that their faith is inadequate or that their doubts have blocked out the healing touch of Christ. Whilst books abound on learning lessons of life through great sufferings, there are many people for whom no answer or lesson has come which makes sense of their hurting. They cry out, but often no answer is given. Having been unemployed for over two years, I can feel for those who see themselves sinking into a depression from which there is no easy escape. I suspect that no Bible verse would bring comfort to those in Hungerford who lost members of their family when one young man took to the streets on a shooting carnage that left eighteen people dead. We believe in a God of love and care, but, when things go wrong, we begin to suspect that that love is not really there. However, many feel that actually to voice this kind of doubt is to fail the test of persevering faith, and so they bottle up inside the wounded feelings they carry. Others simply drift away from their fellowship as there may be no room for their doubts, since they 'rock the boat.' Indeed we must be honest and admit that we ourselves feel some anger, when the good answers we give to help others in their time of trial, are not readily accepted or prove useful. We too often turn away from our failure to help, because we do not know how to go on treating what seems to be a wound that will not be healed.

It is the scope of this book to explore some of the pressures to succeed among Christians, and to see if there is a gospel which embraces and to some degree makes sense of failure. I want to write for Christians of all persuasions but I also want to underline the fact that when we believe in a more immediate experience of the Holy Spirit, as in renewal or charismatic circles, this can actually exacerbate our dilemma when things have gone wrong for us. If we have been baptized with power from on high, how is it that we are not healed or find ourselves so depressed in life? Why has the Spirit not helped us to escape from our problem?

3

Paranoia and Pentecost

Ever since the renewal of interest in the person and work of the Holy Spirit since the 1950s, there have been great moments of blessing, and the so-called 'Toronto' blessing is perhaps only the latest of these. A fresh dynamism has sprung up within the church, producing an appetite for praise and worship and culminating at times in larger celebratory events such as Spring Harvest, Royal Week, the Dales Conventions (representing the 'Restoration' groups in general), and many more. Alongside of these there has sprung up a great number of smaller groups. These range from parish home groups to prayer groups, still the main arena for renewal within the Roman Catholic Church. There has also been a revival of interest in Bible teaching and this has formed a major ingredient of these worship events. Older Christians can well compare these new arrivals with the more established institutions of the Keswick Convention and the Filey Conferences. Perhaps what is different now is the expectation for the Holy Spirit to manifest himself amongst the congregation with a view to releasing charismatic gifts and to facilitate shared ministry such as prayers for healing and deliverance. All this is within the context of a style of worship which is considered to be more flexible in nature and to involve more of a participatory than spectatory element. The common denominator is that there is an expectation for things to happen because the Holy Spirit is at work.

Great Expectations

Of course, it is perfectly legitimate to expect God to be at work in the church by his Holy Spirit, and indeed the Acts of the Apostles reflects a number of these moments. There were days when thousands were converted—moments of sheer power when people were freed from physical illness and demonic bondage. However, here we are reading selective history, not a sequence of daily experiences. Our problems begin when we expect God to give us such events of the Spirit each time we gather together.

I well remember listening to a friend who was a minister of an established denomination. He was sharing his feelings of frustration because nothing was happening in his church. By this he meant that the people were not experiencing charismatic gifts and healing and that the worship was still a diet of old hymns. He was upset because he felt that more was expected of him by his peers, especially now that he had been baptized in the Spirit. He was intolerant with his church, his God and himself. He could not help but compare his output with others and feel that he was failing and they were succeeding. Eventually, he felt obliged to leave his denomination and join a house church because 'they are at least seeing the Spirit at work.' What has begun to emerge within the modern experience of spiritual renewal is a general feeling that certain things should happen as evidence of the Spirit's presence. People should be healed, lives should be changed and the church should be growing in power and freedom in worship. However, the reality is often a hard struggle with little or none of these hopes being realized. There is a period of 'uneventfulness' during which many are tempted to wonder just where they are going wrong. Where have all those promises of spiritual blessings gone? This is the moment when paranoia grips the heart. We begin to imagine that perhaps God is blocking our way forward until we learn a lesson and then he will bless us to our heart's content. Or perhaps we have failed to grasp some basic truth somewhere and if only we look long and hard and listen to those who have achieved the goals for which we long, then we will be given space to move on from the spiritual poverty trap. Sometimes the situation is not helped by attending some large convention where we expect to see demonstrated those events we so deeply covet.

The Need for Integrity

I noticed a couple of years ago a title in a Christian magazine which was 'Not with a Bang but with a Wimber.' The writer was obviously referring to the ministry and work of John Wimber, an American church leader who is well known for his healing ministry and teaching seminars. Many people have attended the various seminars which he and his teams have conducted in the United Kingdom from 1985. They stimulated a very positive and practical approach to praying for healing amongst a wide variety of churches. What the article was trying to voice was that a number of people found life in the local church a very different reality from that of the large seminars, and wondered therefore about the genuineness of the ministry which had been given. I for one attended the Acts '86 convention which was held at the NEC complex outside Birmingham. The teaching sessions on healing were by far the best attended and they were conducted sensitively and there was indeed evidence of a powerful work of healing going on during the sessions. What was interesting was that John Wimber mentioned that he had prayed and worked for the release of a healing ministry within his church and for a year saw no fruit for his labours in this direction. He said that during this time he personally learnt integrity of heart and then gradually a healing ministry followed. Perhaps this is a clue to the way forward in our discussion; we need to learn integrity in our walk in this spirit of Pentecost. In our desire for eventfulness we all too often become a sort of religious clone trying to reproduce in our world the ministry of some other. We need to maintain our genuineness and go forward in our journey with God as he directs. We cannot even ape the blessings of God. We must walk in them for themselves.

A further contribution to this illness of the spirit is the oversimplified summaries of what to expect from God. There are the prosperity doctrines which teach that, if we give sacrificially to God, he will in turn ensure that we have blessings in abundance. A common text employed here is that of Malachi 3.10:

'"Bring all the tithes into the storehouse, that there may be food in my house. Test me in this," says the Lord, "and see if I will not throw open the flood-gates of heaven and pour out so much blessing that you will not have room enough for it."' (NIV)

However, it is glibly assumed that the blessings in question are material in na-ture. This is in sharp contrast to the hard times of the life of the New Testament church and its frequent appeals for financial help. On more than one occasion leaders representing some of the emerging renewal groups have sought to en-courage their congregations by saying that Christians are 'children of the King.' By this is meant that our life-style should be substantial, befitting the high stand-ards of the well-off. Well, we are indeed privileged children, but our King had nowhere to lay his head. All too often our theology is simply so bad that we distort the word, and the truth is not in us.

Praise and Reality

There is also the teaching that by praising God for everything and persisting in this endeavour, then God will bring blessing out of any circumstance. There is no doubt that the Scriptures have commanded us to 'give thanks in all cir-cumstances, for this is God's will for you in Christ Jesus' (1 Thess 5.18). Merlin C. Carothers in his best selling books, the first of which was entitled *From Prison to Praise*, goes one step further and reminds us that the Bible also encourages us to give thanks to God 'for' all things as well as 'in' all things (cf. Eph 5.20). In his books he gives a number of challenging examples of people who suffered great tragedies but who praised God for what had happened, believing that God's will was in the event and that he was in control of it all. One of these examples concerns a Christian women who married an alcoholic. For many years the wife struggled to raise their two children and suffered great anxiety and hardships. The husband indulged in a life-time of petty crime and was eventually impris-oned. The now-destitute wife finally decided to divorce her husband and try to raise her children in a more stable environment. Upon reading a copy of *From Prison to Praise* she decided to try and improve her life by giving thanks to God for her husband's life and alcoholism.

'"Thank you for Al and his drinking," she prayed "Thank you for the years of poverty and fear and loneliness."'[3]

The account goes on to say how the husband was later converted and the cou-ple went on to remarry and lead a new life through faith in Christ. The implica-tion is that, by this process of praise, God will make things succeed for us. However, the danger in this kind of teaching is that we make praise a tool in itself, a technique to achieve our own goals. For surely, it is hardly correct for a Christian to praise God for evil and the damage that people do to others? Many have tried this praising route to freedom and have almost shipwrecked their

---

3 Merlin R Carothers, *Power in Praise* (Coverdale House Publishers, 1974) p 75.

faith. One could almost write about this and call it 'from praise to prison!' It is worth remembering that, far from giving his Father thanks for the sins of the city, Jesus wept when he thought about the people in Jerusalem. As Christians we are surely called upon to praise God for all he is and does amongst us and yes, he can make use of all our times of hurt, not because we praise him for them, but because he is a sovereign God; he can choose to do so. It is as we cast all our cares upon him, that we experience our need of him and realize again that he cares for us (1 Peter 5.7).

Faith and Healing

We have already touched upon the subject of sickness. This is only a problem of failure in those churches which not only teach and practise a healing ministry, but who emphasize that Jesus wants us to be healed. This is because we are struck with the fact that there are always those who remain unhealed. Have they thwarted Jesus' plan for their lives by their lack of faith or by some secret sin? The real problem is that such churches have not left any room for failure in their doctrine. And so a reason must be found to 'let Jesus off the hook' and the reason usually takes the form of finding fault with the sufferer or of detecting the work of the Devil. Either way, the end-product is a neatness whereby no mystery or failure upsets the belief.

Yet this is simply not true of the biblical accounts. After the wonder of creation comes the horror of rebellion in paradise. The history of God's chosen people is not too proud a one. Great heroes like Noah are found drunk and disorderly and a man after God's own heart like King David commits murder in order to cover up his adultery. These are certainly not white-washed characters. Perhaps the book which most shows up this reluctance to deal openly and objectively with failure is the book of Job. I have thought that his comforters (or counsellors) were at their most effective and helpful when they remained silent. There was a sense in the book that Job could voice his anxieties more openly as a result of this. However, once they opened their mouths, Job was in even more difficulties. The writer puts upon their lips the classic Old Testament doctrine that suffering or failure was due to sins previously committed. And so they trotted out their formulae and became more irate when Job simply did not agree with them. The story then shifts into a number of rounds by which the friends become more and more wild in their opinions as to Job's reasons for his dilemma and state that worse is in store if he does not accept the truth as they see it. It becomes more apparent as the story continues that the counsellors are much more concerned to maintain their beliefs and so keep failure at a manageable level; Job's sufferings now assume a minor importance in the story.

4   *Gateway to Hope* (Fount Paperbacks, 1985) pp 37ff.

Prophetic Failure

The biblical picture goes a step further on this issue by underlining how some of God's faithful men were called to experience only limited success and a great deal of heartache and failure. Maria Boulding speaks of the prophetic failure of the eighth century prophets.[4] Isaiah was informed at his call to ministry that the response to his work would be a hardening of the heart and a growing disinterest among the populace (Is 6.8-10). Hardly an encouraging start, and yet a realistic one. Jeremiah did not fare much better and even suffered imprisonment for his faithfulness and ended his days in obscurity and exile amongst a people he obviously did not like (see Jer 43.1-7). He is often called the moaning prophet, perhaps unfairly. He freely expresses his hurt feelings to God and yet he goes on with his work and from time to time flashes of vision come to him of a day when, despite the odds, God will have a faithful remnant at last who will acknowledge their God.

'O Lord, you deceived me, and I was deceived; you overpowered me and prevailed. I am ridiculed all day long, everyone mocks me…; So the word of the Lord has brought me insult and reproach all day long…: But the Lord is with me like a mighty warrior…Sing to the Lord! Give praise to the Lord! He rescues the life of the needy from the hands of the wicked.'   (Jer 20.7-13)

'"The time is coming," declares the Lord, "when I will make a new covenant with the house of Israel and with the house of Judah…I will be their God and they will be my people. No longer will a man teach his neighbour, or a man his brother, saying, 'Know the Lord,' because they will all know me from the least of them to the greatest."'   (Jer 31.31-34)

Space prevents us from looking in similar depth into the planned but failed marriage of Hosea and how God used this to illustrate the relationship of Israel with Yahweh their God. It is interesting to note that, when Jesus was summarizing the general reaction to the prophetic ministry, he talked in terms of the people stoning them. We have the benefit of hindsight and see how their words were like seeds planted in the ground and now provide us with a rich treasury of guidance, but they themselves were not so fortunate. Similarly, in our failure we may not see any point to it all, but this is when we are especially to voice how it feels and trust our lives into hands more capable than our own.

Failure in the Early Church

The New Testament reveals that, even after the Pentecost event and whilst the church was still young, it encountered its failures. Paul ended his days in prison confinement and probably never saw Spain as he had hoped (Rom 15.24). Peter may have escaped miraculously from prison as a result of prayer but the saintly James was beheaded with the sword, his days of promise rudely cut down. The writer to the Hebrews when reviewing the church in general gives a list of those who lived by faith. What is remarkable is that he gives a list of those who both triumphed against all the odds by faith and those who had faith to fail, by the world's standards. He is anxious to stress the fact that it is the same faith at work in both circumstances. He underlines the importance of both experiences by saying that one is not complete without the other:

'These were all commended for their faith, yet none of them received what had been promised. God had planned something better for us so that *only together with us* would they be made perfect.' (Heb 11.39-40)

And so the picture of a perfected church is only complete when the winners and the losers are able to share the journey of their faith together. The writer is actually telling us that we need failure as part of the real story of what is the Christian lot. Where better is this union of success and failure demonstrated than in the life of Jesus himself? His incarnation included an element of planned failure. God was taking risks through his Son and for the first time, Jesus would personally experience some of the failures of being in a human society. In the wonder of heaven the Christ enjoyed such unity and harmony within the Godhead; on earth he would know the rejection of men, he would fail to win all their love. John tells us that 'He came to that which was his own, but his own did not receive him' (John 1.11). This was a new hurt for Jesus and was to characterize his earthly ministry. He would learn rejection and the limitation of his power. The Christ of glory would feel tired and jaded and drink the cup of depression in the garden of Gethsemane. This would be no cosmetic Christ, he was going to look almost twice his age before he died (John 8.57). Surely the writer to the Hebrews is making this point when he says that 'although he was a son, he learned obedience from what he suffered.' (Heb 5.8). Jesus was sinless, and yet had lessons of obedience to learn through suffering. This obedience was even unto death, death on a cross.

4
The Cross and the Domino Theory

'The other gods were strong, but thou wast weak;
They rode, but thou didst stagger to a throne.

But to our wounds only God's wounds can speak,
And not a god has wounds but Thou alone.'[5]

The domino theory states the political belief that if one country falls to an expansionist power, the next or neighbouring countries will inevitably fall in turn. The cross is like such a theory; once we fall under its power, then it will leave a trail right through our understanding of Christian hope and expectation. For example, even when Jesus was enjoying the heights of success, he kept his eye on his appointment with the cross. In the middle of great moments he deliberately prepared his disciples for its crushing effects. It was one such occasion as this that prompted Peter to say to Jesus that he would not allow him to suffer such a humiliating defeat. He was enjoying the sweetness of success; God the Father had revealed to him the very nature of Jesus and it was a gloriously enjoyable moment. And so Peter speaks out from the perspective of success. But Jesus decided to awaken him rudely to the cross, and so startled Peter with the words 'Get behind me, Satan; you are a stumbling block to me' (Matt 16.21-23). According to Matthew a similar moment occurs for Peter some time later at the time of the transfiguration of Jesus on the mount. Something of the glory of Christ shone out on that high mountain and suddenly there was the conversation of the saints, Moses and Elijah, in dialogue with Jesus. Peter is carried away with the great event and immediately makes plans to capitalize upon it; but all is brushed aside. Jesus seals the occasion with more words about his suffering and death (Matt 17.1-13). On both of these peaks of success, Jesus introduces the focus of the cross. Then the domino theory goes to work in the hearts of his disciples. Everything else must align itself with this dominant theme. Every success must be surrendered to the cross; after all, in order to follow Christ, we are commanded to take up our cross, not our successes.

Paul Tournier speaks of the cross as the proof of God through failure:
'But after the miracles in Galilee there comes the solitude of the cross. After the proof of God by success, there comes the proof of God in failure; a paradoxical proof, but how much greater, in fact, and more absolute, despite its apparently relative character.'[6]

Tournier is underlining the need for witness of the Spirit in order to sustain growth and development of faith. However, he wants to understand times of

5 E Shillito, *Jesus of the Scars.*   **6** *The Person Reborn* (SCM Press, 1977) p 33.

power as relative and the weakness of the cross as absolute to this witness. It is no good being sustained by our experiences of power, because even John the Baptist was taken from his public successes and confined to a prison where his doubts assailed him. So we must fasten our faith not on the day of Pentecost, but on the fact of the cross.

The Last Domino

And yet there is another aspect to the cross as a domino which we must consider. It was F. W. Boreham, an evangelical and contemplative writer from the earlier period of the twentieth century, who first suggested this idea to me. He pointed out that the winner of this game is the first one to lay down his last domino tile. So the cross is the last piece which God laid down in his plan of salvation. Jesus echoed this fact in his dying words 'It is finished!' Therefore, the cross with all its sense of abandonment and pain, also marks a way forward. For Jesus, as well as for us, it is not the end of the story. We know this with hindsight; Jesus knew it because he was the resurrection and the life. The cross now becomes the ultimate focus through which we see God's love in Christ. It tells us that the pathway for us to return to holiness of life is through this door. The writer to the Hebrews paints this very picture when he says:

> 'And so Jesus also suffered outside the city gate to make the people holy through his own blood. Let us, then, go to him outside the camp, bearing the disgrace he bore.' (Heb 13.12-13)

And because it is the final piece for God to play, it is also the harbinger of the end; the fulfilling of the Kingdom of God. The coming of the Spirit at Pentecost was only the beginning of this process of completion. And so Pentecost then, cannot be separated from the Spirit of the cross. To seek the Spirit without the cross is to stalk the great events of success and power for their own sake and that is idolatry. It is seeking after self-satisfaction. To take the cross and all its apparent failure but not realise that it is God's final move in the plan of salvation is to empty it of its power and leave no room for growing through failure.

A Failure that Heals

Maria Boulding draws these two dimensions of power and powerlessness together and says that the cross therefore becomes a vehicle for healing:

> 'If you have ever been sickened by the crumbling of some enterprise into which you had put all your best effort and love of your heart, you are caught up into the fellowship of Christ's death and resurrection...God has dealt wth our failure by himself becoming a failure in Jesus Christ and so healing it from inside.'[7]

It is a place of brokenness as well as a place for picking up the broken pieces and moving on in the spiritual journey. Kosuke Koyama tells us that the cross is not

---

7 *Gateway to Hope, ibid* p 9.

a bridge, for that is a symbol of transition from one side to another. It is rather an image of intersection where a number of roads meet. As such it gives a feeling of confrontation, encounter and conflict. It is a point at which people meet, and it stands for a painful solution.[8] The cross then, offers us a unique failure, for it is one where hope meets with despair. Out of its crushing embrace comes an openness to a future. For the moment, let us look at what we can learn from Christ's experience of the cross and the way it enters into human failures.

The Cry and the Silence

'Jesus cried out in a loud voice, "My God, my God, why have you forsaken me?"' (Matt 27.46)

'And when Jesus had cried out again in a loud voice, he gave up his spirit.' (Matt 27.50)

The most obvious point about Jesus crying is that he received no answer to his question. There was only the sound of his cry of dereliction. Not even his somewhat limited number of hostile on-lookers understood his cry. They thought he was calling for Elijah to return, which many considered to be the moment which would announce the return of the Messiah. In other words they thought his pain was pushing him into hysteria and they sought to ease his lot with the sponge of vinegar. However, the question was necessary and genuine enough. He was experiencing the alienation of a sinful humanity and this was entirely new to him. The anxiety of separation was immense and an answer was called for. His cry once and for all reveals that the question of suffering exists and that we can live with the question even when it is not answered.

Therefore, Jesus is united with everyone whose cry is given no answer. He is with us to tell us that it is really all right to give the hurt a voice. This in itself can be the beginning of healing. All too often we bottle up our rage and anger, fearing that to speak it out is to incur the displeasure of the Almighty. What amazes me about Job is that he takes on God with his complaint and that at the end of the day he is commended for his integrity. Jesus may have been silent before his accusers at his trial but on the cross he cries out.

Some time ago I was sharing counselling with a single woman who was trying to come to terms with her depression. She was a nurse and had been interviewed a number of times by her GP and had been taking some tablets to stimulate her emotions a little. However, she continued to slide into her feelings of anxiety. We shared together on a number of occasions and they largely took the form of my asking a question, the response to which would be a long silence followed by a muted and generalized answer. For example when I asked her how she got on with her father, she struggled for some twenty minutes to say 'all right.' Clearly, there was much more not yet said but I did not feel it proper

---

8 Kosuke Koyama, *Three Mile an Hour God* (SCM Press, 1979) p 42.

to push unduly for a fuller answer. One day I asked her to tell me how it felt to just go home as she did periodically, and walk up the garden path and knock on the door, after which it would be opened by her father. Again there followed the long and silent struggle and then slowly she began to cry. What began as a series of sighs soon developed into a rapid flow of tears and emotion, increasing in intensity and lasting for about twenty minutes or more.

Needless to say, I did not interrupt. Afterwards she began to share quite freely how she had been mistreated and made to feel unwanted at home. Being able to cry she found refreshing, because it was giving voice to all the denied feelings she had acquired. Her cry was affirming to herself and it freed her to confront her own hurt and choose to go forward from there. It was by no means a pleasant experience, but it did prove to be a healing one. And so the cross invites us to join Jesus in his cry and not be discouraged if no answer comes. It is enough to have asked the question. Just as Jesus was trusted with silence, so are we. Again we could go on and talk about the perspective of the resurrection for the cry on the cross, but we only appreciate this because we have seen the next chapter even as we read this one. Our next chapter is not yet written and so, rather than trying to squeeze in some answer that might ease the pain, there is often only the choice to believe that our cry has been heard and that that is enough for now.

Jesus did in fact go one more step than this, he surrendered his cry. He gave up his spirit into the hands of his Father because he had finished what he had to do and say. Here he precedes the ranks of those who were to follow him who had faith to give up, to let go. Once the cry had been shouted there was no grabbing back or holding on to the hurt. It was all to be surrendered. Neither did he attempt to explain to those around him the meaning of his failure because he had committed his cry to a stronger hand: his powerlessness was put into a hand more powerful still. And so, as we focus on this cross, we are free to shout out our loud cries and then surrender the moment to God and begin to face a future. It is time to move on. We must leave behind all speculation about 'why.' The scream has been heard, now we must surrender to hope and look to a tomorrow with God still with us.

The Naked Failure

'And they crucified him. Dividing up his clothes, they cast lots to see what each would get.'   (Mark 15.24)

'Those who passed by hurled insults at him.'   (Mark 15.29)

'Jesus answered him, "I tell you the truth, today you will be with me in paradise."'   (Luke 23.43)

For many, the Christ who hung naked on the cross was a far cry from being the King of the Jews. Like the fable of the emperor who paraded in public without his clothes, Jesus now became something almost like a joke. So he was mocked and insulted because he had not lived up to the promise of power and glory. There is something ugly about human nature when its heroes seem to fail them. The hero becomes the target and is dethroned from his importance and exposed, made naked in the glare of public rejection. And Jesus is no exception, he bears the brunt of public disapproval. He had not lived up to public demand and thrown out the Roman oppressor. He had not allowed himself to be made king by popular acclaim. He had upset the spiritual leaders by challenging them to be more committed to caring for their fellows than to maintaining their elevated status in the public eye. Now both of these groups had combined and turned against him. Christ's failure to please had brought him to nakedness of the cross.

But there was also something common about this naked Christ. He was treated like all others defeated in battle in the ancient world. He was stripped and marched into captivity. It was an act of dispossession and humiliation on the part of the victor. Being captured on the cross in this way, Jesus enters into the lot of all those who are robbed and reduced to nothing by their failure in society. It means that he has already experienced the horror of the death camps where millions were herded, naked into the gas chambers. It also means that he knows how it feels to be as nothing before others.

Naked and Vulnerable

Being naked also means having nothing to give. It is to be in the place of vulnerability with no place to hide. Jesus would not even hide behind the anaesthesia of the sponge with its wine and myrrh, and he would not escape his nakedness in sleep. This was his choice for us, for in doing this he identifies with all those who feel that their failure is open to the critical eyes of others and feel there is no escape from shame and embarrassment. It is at times like this that we feel worthless and want to hide. Such hurt crushes our faith and we are in danger of giving up. We become hard and the mention of such things, even long after the event, still leaves us feeling sore.

I well remember talking with a friend in the late 1960s about an experience that caused him and his wife much pain. As a result he was on the verge of giving up his ministry altogether. He had been the minister of his church for five years, and in that denomination this was the time for his re-election process. What made the whole thing even more upsetting was that he and his wife both had to sit silently through, as various church leaders discussed his merits or otherwise. Harsh criticisms were made of his failure to bring in more new people to the church. After a fairly heated discussion a vote was taken, and he was narrowly re-elected by two votes. He said that he was left with the feeling that he had been stripped bare in front of everyone and had not the space to defend or speak for himself.

There are many who live with this kind of failure and it can be like a hurt that will not go away. Yet Jesus while choosing to stay awake also chose to remain silent about himself. Words at times like these seem quite useless. Jesus left his vindication to another and we must go the same way if we would be people of the cross. Our hurting must not be allowed to make us hard, we must share our failure with the man on the cross and wait for the hope that will not leave us ashamed of our failure. I like the poem of Amy Wilson Carmichael which encourages us to stay open to the cross and, like Jesus, despise its shame;

> From prayer that asks that I may be
> Sheltered from winds that beat on Thee,
> From fearing when I should aspire,
> From faltering when I should climb higher,
> From silken self, O captain, free
> Thy soldier who would follow Thee.
>
> From subtle love of softening things,
> From easy choices, weakenings,
> (Not thus are spirits fortified,
> Not this way went the Crucified)
> From all that dims Thy Calvary,
> O Lamb of God, deliver me.
>
> Give me the love that leads the way,
> The faith that nothing can dismay,
> The hope no disappointments tire,
> The passion that will burn like fire,
> Let me not sink to be a clod:
> Make me Thy fuel, Flame of God.[9]

Christ's nakedness is a call to openness for us as well as a recognition that we can live with those moments when we feel we have nothing to offer. Yet out of this nothingness, Jesus offers us everything. Paradoxical as it may seem, hanging naked before the world, Jesus promises paradise to the next man who sees his own nakedness and failure. Silent before his accusers, Jesus now speaks out and when he does it is to make an offer of more to come. Truly despair and hope meet at the cross. It is a reminder that we should not be too attached to succeeding in this world as we are journeying to a more permanent home in the paradise of God. This is not escapism, it is being aware that we should not became preoccupied with being a success nor become enmeshed in failure or in worry about what others will then think of us. Both are a cul-de-sac on earth but Christ promises us paradise.

The third man hanging there also wanted a paradise but his was cheap. He first wanted setting free from his predicament and then to enter into promise. For Jesus and the other who would follow him, it was by the way of death. So

9   Amy Carmichael.

for us, there is no easy escape from our failure, we must taste a death if we would see life. It may look and feel messy to all concerned, but for us it is our choice to make ourselves available to a future. We may have to die to all kinds of cherished hopes and ambitions and yet the cross is just the place to do this.

> *Suffering*
> See what a transformation!
> Those hands so active and powerful
> Now are tied, alone and fainting,
> You see where your work ends.
> But you are confident still, and gladly commit
> what is rightful into a stronger hand,
> and say that you are contented.
> You were free for a moment of bliss,
> then you yielded your freedom into the hand of Glory,
> That he might perfect it in glory.

> *Death*
> Come now, highest of feasts
> on the way to freedom eternal;
> death, strike off the fetters,
> break down the walls that oppress us,
> our bedazzled soul and ephemeral body,
> what we may see at the last sight
> which here was not vouchsafed us.[10]

Darkness

> 'It was now about the sixth hour, and darkness came over the whole land until the ninth hour, for the sun stopped shining. Jesus called out in a loud voice "Father, into your hands I commit my spirit."'   (Luke 23.44-46)

So Jesus hangs in the dark and finds it to be the end of his journey. Exhausted and thirsty, he dies. In a curious way he is both the centre of attention and at the same time is lost from view. The darkness separates him from even the few who were there for him. Darkness seems to underline the feelings of isolation and loneliness that all people experience and here Jesus makes his exit. There is no shining light, no band of angels comforting him; he dies almost hid from view. As well as the public side of failure there is also the private world where our thoughts and feelings surround us. Not many can enter this place with us. We may brood and cry alone or wallow in guilt. It is our choice to shut others out as failure, like darkness, cuts us off from others. There often comes a point when our sense of worthlessness is too great to carry before others, and so we retreat into shadow; we abide alone. This is often the most powerful time and the most

---

10 Dietrich Bonhoeffer, *The Way to Freedom* (Collins, 1966) pp 16, 19.

dangerous. It is in this place of separation that we make decisions about what is to do next. The darkness that descends upon us can rob us of any vision for the future and turn us in upon ourselves. Jesus has indeed, gone this way before us. He was like a grain of wheat which for a moment was abiding alone, but then he turned to the Father and, for the first and only time in his life, learnt to die.

Jesus in darkness made a commitment to his Father and handed over his spirit. I think this was a supreme act of trust because he knew there was a future through his death. Though in darkness, he did not lose his perspective of the future. To many it seemed to be an ignominious end and futile at that. And we must not be in a hurry to plunder the cross and rob it of its importance with some empty triumphalism. For example, there is always the danger in popular evangelical theology, whilst wishing to underline the accomplished work of the cross and its victory, to paint a Christ who was in control of the events. The darkness tells us he was not. Here Jesus tastes the loneliness of all who know what it is to be defeated and pushed away into the dark by the more powerful. His pain and isolation he felt first for himself and then for all. The cross, while being a real victory over the world, the flesh and the Devil, is precisely so because it is also the place where all failure is fully embraced and redeemed.

Failure and a Future

The cross then brings together all our failures but also points the way forward to the possibility of a salvation which will win our failure. And so the cross is the tree of shame but it can also be the tree of life. It seems that two spiritualities meet here and complement one another; the contemplative and the charismatic, that of suffering and that of conquest.

> Two trees
> proclaim in spring
> a word to the world.
>
> One exploding
> into blossom
> trumpets glory
>
> One stretching
> dead limbs
> holds the empty
> body of God
>
> Both speak
> with due reserve
> into the listening
> ear of the world. [11]

11 Ralph Wright *Life is Simpler Towards Evening* (Francestown: Golden Quill Press, 1983) p 64.

the spirit of Pentecost outpoured upon the earth, there is the need to be reminded of the perspective of the cross. Otherwise, they chase after the Spirit and search for eventfulness, but there is an inability to work with failed expectations; they have not understood the cross. For those who contemplate the sufferings of the cross and remain there, there is the need for the Spirit to show them the possibilities of new growth. Or else there is only the expectation of suffering and its lessons and little room for the Holy Spirit to bring fresh initiatives and renewed vitality of life. Calvary contains statements of both failure and future and we need to hold both in balance if we are to handle both our victories and defeats.

_____

5

Gaining from Losing

It was C. S. Lewis who said, 'Cynicism is the occupational hazard of every serious thinking Christian.' He was underlining the mood which so often robs us of the will to go on in our spiritual journey when things have gone wrong. There are those times when we receive no answer nor can see any sense to be gained from our failure, but we still have to choose whether to give up or go on. Even without an answer to the question 'why?' are there any gains to be made or do we give in to cynicism and say there is no point? There are indeed some basic lessons of life to be learned but they may not necessarily bring us the healing we may be seeking. However, they do help us to let go of the dead end to which our failures bring us and to hold on to a God who promises a tomorrow.

The Power of Helplessness
> O Lord,
> remember not only the men and women of goodwill,
> but those of ill will.
> But do not remember all the suffering
> they have inflicted upon us;
> remember the fruits we have brought
> thanks to this suffering—
> our comradeship, our loyalty, our humility, our courage,
> our generosity, the greatness of heart
> which has grown out of all this;
> and when they come to judgment,
> let all the fruits which we have borne be their forgiveness.

(Found beside the body of a dead child at Ravensbruck concentration camp).

'Human helplessness is the crucible out of which victory could rise.'[12] So wrote Catherine Marshall after rebuilding her life following the tragic death of her husband, Peter, when he was only 47 years of age. She felt so totally inadequate to manage her life and that of a baby son. However, her sense of insufficiency led her to the 'inexhaustible sufficiency of God.'[13] Finding God's availability in a time of failure she described as the power of helplessness. It is such times of crisis which make us aware of our need to recover dependence upon God. The doctrines of success lead us inevitably to the sense of our own self-sufficiency, and this is nothing short of idolatry. Standing in direct contrast to this idea are the words of Jesus, 'Without me, you can do nothing' (John 15.5). Dr. Arthur Gossip, some years ago, described this as the most hopeful words in scripture. 'For it is on the basis of the frank recognition of our utter fecklessness apart from Him that Christ enters into covenant with us, and gives us His tremendous promises.'[14] Whilst we are not wanting to undermine the strengths of the individual, there is the constant need to learn dependence upon the grace of God.

There is an episode in Paul Gallico's novel *The Poseidon Affair* where a stricken ship is sinking and two clergymen find themselves responding to the panic amongst the passengers. One is young and determined and gathers around him a group of strong people who make a bid to escape from the ship. Before leaving, he notices the older clergyman sitting down with the depressed passengers who had obviously given up all hope of getting out. 'Why don't you save yourself and join us?' he asks. The older priest replies, 'You only have a gospel for the strong. Where is your good news for the weak? I will stay here with the hopeless; at least they will know that they have not been abandoned.'

Confession and Forgiveness

We can still find good news when we are weak, for God is for us too. For some, this recognition can only come with failure. Something else we can learn from our helplessness is that of confession and forgiveness. Confession is not only a recognition and acceptance of our failure, it is also an awareness that we can go free. It means that we do not have to live in judgment. Confession means that our failure is acceptable to God.

'The sacrifice acceptable to God is a broken spirit, a broken and contrite heart,
O God, you will not despise.' (Psalm 51.17)
Maria Boulding speaks of the Spirit of God having to batter through our proud defences in order to awaken us to the need of forgiveness. This is what is called the work of contrition whereby the bruised heart is set free for its lover.[15] We are once again on the road to recovery and wholeness as forgiveness brings us back to needing God's love. It is this truth which Mother Basiliea Schlink expounded

---

12 Catherine Marshall, *Beyond Ourselves* (Hodder and Stoughton, 1972) p 153.
13 *Ibid* p 155.
14 *The Interpreter's Bible*, (Edinburgh: Thomas Nelson & Sons Ltd, 1953-54).
15 *Ibid* p 110.

in her book *Repentance, the Joy-filled Life*. She underlines that it is as we repent that the Kingdom of God is at hand for us and that is the ultimate joy of living with God.[16] This is unfortunately a spirituality which is all too absent from Evangelical theology. This approach to repentance lies at the heart of penance in the Catholic Rite. Here, it is a commitment to work at and to grow from accepting our failure and surrendering it back to God. What is more, as Christians we have to live in the open with our failure. Hence penance has become a shared experience with the emergence of the Lent season as the church's celebration of failure in the light of an Easter rising that is about to come. It is a time to learn anew the joy of sins forgiven. To love God therefore involves a personal suffering. Even God the Father counted the cost to bring us his love.

Giving Way to God

If the ground is well dug by troubles, persecutions, detractions and infirmities—they are few who ascend so high without this—if it be well broken up by great detachment from all self-interest, it will drink in so much water that it can hardly be parched again...

Tears gain everything, and one drop of water attracts another,

(Teresa of Avila)[17]

Chuck Colson, the former White House aide to President Nixon, said on television in 1985 that it was through the failures of the Watergate scandal and his own imprisonment that he began to experience God's presence and love in his life. His time in jail led him to reflect upon how his seeming self-sufficiency had in fact been his undoing. Since then he had gained a new perspective to life; it was that he should live for God and so crown Jesus as Lord. Failure had brought him to salvation. The most important lesson of any person's life is to learn that God wants a personal relationship with us. This takes priority over any useful service that we may offer Him.

My goal is God himself,
not joy, nor peace,
Nor even blessing,
but himself, my God;
'Tis thine to lead me there—
not mine, but His—
At any cost, dear Lord,
by any road.' (F. Brook)

Often we are so busy trying to be a success for God and others that we forget this. Failure is used by God to bring us back to basics. We discover our inad-

16 *Repentance - The Joy-filled Life* (Oliphants, 1969).
17 Sister Mary ODC (ed), *Living Water* (DLT, 1985) p 24.

equacy and limitations and they become the tools to teach us the Lordship of Christ. It is this displacement of the self for God that restores the balance of our lives.

Getting a Better Perspective

I asked God for strength, that I might achieve;
I was made weak, that I might learn humbly to obey.
I asked for health, that I might do greater things;
I was given infirmity, that I might do better things.
I asked for riches, that I might be happy;
I was given poverty, that I might be wise.
I asked for power, that I might have the praise of men;
I was given weakness, that I might feel the need of God.
I asked for all things that I might enjoy life;
I was given life that I might enjoy all things.
I got nothing that I asked for—
but everything I had hoped for.
Almost, despite myself, my
unspoken prayers were answered.
I am among all men, most richly blessed.

(Anonymous Confederate soldier)

There is a very interesting statement of Joseph's when he finally confronted his brothers from his strength as the Prime Minister of Egypt: 'You intended to harm me, but God intended it for good, to accomplish what is now being done, the saving of many lives' (Gen 50.20). They had plotted to get rid of him but God used Joseph's failure to secure a future for his family. So now, years later, Joseph had a better perspective of what had gone wrong in his life. Our failures may well dash our hopes but they also leave us no option but to trust God and that he will give us a new perspective on the event. This may, like Joseph, take years, but we could come to understand why God allowed or even engineered our failures.

6
Conclusion

Failures then, more readily than successes, teach us to embrace the whole of our humanity and own ourselves without pretence before God. Successes may lead us to believe that of course God must accept us now, look how he is blessing us! Failure tells us that God has accepted me anyway for he sent Jesus to taste my failure at Calvary. I am acceptable to God on no other basis than that he has demonstrated his acceptance of me already. And this cross reminds us of the balance we must maintain on the spiritual journey; it is rather like a see-saw. If we would go up and gain the heights in life, then at the same time we must plunge downward into the dust of failure. Both the heights and the depths together give us the balance we need for growth.

> I do not deny
> that once one becomes a Christian
> in every sense,
> one just about asks
> for crucifixion.
>
> But where there is Calvary
> there is an Easter.
> Or it is not Calvary at all.
> It is just suicide.
> The Christian, like the Church itself,
> is always growing.
> Crucifixion is nothing more
> than the cry of breath.
> Pilgrim do not be afraid of the cross;
> It is a glorious cross.
>
> (C. W. Jones)